UNBREAKABLE

UNBREAKABLE

The Secret to Developing an Indomitable Spirit

SIFU KARL ROMAIN

Protégé Consulting Group, LLC

Nanuet, New York

Copyright © 2017 by Sifu Karl Romain

All rights reserved. No part of this publication may be reproduced, distributed or transmitted in any form or by any means, without prior written permission.

Sifu Karl Romain/Protégé Consulting Group, LLC
P.O. Box 372
Nanuet, New York/10954

www.daylighttraining.com

This work is partially memoir and partially instructional. The author shares events from his life and has done his best to recall them factually. The self-help information presented has been learned from many sources and is used in the author's private coaching practice. The contents are offered as a source of inspiration and practical advice, but the results of using this information will depend on the reader's application. The author and publisher hereby disclaim any liability to any party for any loss, damage, or disruption caused by errors or omissions, and shall not be liable for any damages.

Unbreakable / Sifu Karl Romain. -- 1st ed.

ISBN 978- 1548168841

*To my children
Hope and Isaiah*

I hope this book and the example I set for you inspire you to live the life of your dreams and be unbreakable.

—LOVE, DAD

Contents

Foreword xi
Introduction 1
Growth Through Challenge 11
The Secret Of Success 21
    The Story of My Success 25
    Developing Self-Confidence 34
6 Principles To RESET And Become Unbreakable 47
    RESET Principle #1 – Truth 50
    RESET Principle #2 – Thoughts 60
    RESET Principle #3 – Purpose 62
    RESET Principle #4 – Choice 66
    RESET Principle #5 – Action 78
    RESET Principle #6 – Accountability 81
To Begin, Just Breathe 84
Unbreakable Legacy 89
    A Legacy of Love 91
Final Thoughts 99
Want Help Becoming Unbreakable? 101
About The Author 103

Acknowledgments

This book would not be possible if it were not for the many outstanding teachers and mentors I have had over the course of my life. I am grateful to them all. The lessons and exercises presented here have come from many sources, and some have been developed from a combination of the techniques I have learned.

I would like to thank Fred Mertens, Lauren Sage, Reuben Prett, Keith Cooke, Eric Chen, Berry Fowler, Master Phill Sant, Master Willy Lin, Master Leon Tresscott, Richard Branden, Tai Lopez, Dave Meltzer, Karen Hoyos, and Master George Crayton, Jr.

In addition to my teachers, there are many people who have helped with the creation of this book, and for that, I'd like to thank Allison Jones, Jacqui Phillips, Lika Kvirikashvili, Erica Page, Manu Bains, Maridelle Cajucom, Melissa Marshall, Angie DeAngelis and my daughter, Hope Romain.

Special thanks to Veronica, Fabiola, Pierre, Chin family, Brown family and the members of the Edgewater Kung Fu Academy Family.

Foreword

Sifu Karl Romain is a world champion martial artist and a world champion human being who has dedicated his life to helping others to reach their highest level of personal success and fulfillment. He also happens to be one of the nicest people I have ever met.

Over the past forty years, I have had the good fortune to have met and worked with thousands of big hearted individuals with a genuine desire to help others. As the founder of Sylvan Learning Centers, I found it easy to recruit a team of caring professionals, mostly former classroom teachers, to help solve a huge problem in our country—way too many nice kids were struggling in school, falling further and further behind, simply because they lacked the basic skills and confidence to succeed. More recently, when I founded the Fowler International Academy of Professional Coaching and began training and certifying life and business coaches, I once again became surrounded by passionate individuals dedicated to serving others. And that is how I first met Sifu, as a student in our Certified Professional Coach course.

Early on it became obvious Sifu was going to become a superstar. An avid learner, he excelled in every course we offered and has earned our highest credentials in life, business, and executive leadership coaching. He was so driven by his unwavering mission to help others, we invited Sifu to join our team and he became a Certified Master Trainer. We now refer to him as "everyone's favorite master teacher".

Since then, Sifu and I collaborated on various projects and initiatives and became much more than just colleagues; we have become friends. So, when I was asked to write the foreword for his newest book, I found it to be an honor and a pleasure.

If you are looking to take the next step in improving your life, and the lives of those closest to you, this beautifully written book is your guide to becoming unbreakable. Through personal stories, inspirational messages and practical life-enhancing exercises, you will be motivated to reset your life and get started on your path to achieving personal and professional greatness.

As you read the following pages, you will learn how to take a complete and objective inventory of your life as it is today. You will discover simple, easy-to-implement steps to making immediate changes that will help you feel more confident and better equipped to embrace the life of your dreams. You'll learn techniques like forgiving yourself and others for past indiscretions and how to rid yourself of the emotional burdens that come from guilt, shame, and resentment. You'll gain insight into what really makes you happy and you will develop a clearer understanding of your true purpose in life.

Most of all, Unbreakable will reach you at your core. It will allow you to release the unique and wonderful spirit that is the essence of who you are and guide you toward achieving the full potential that lies within.

I hope you enjoy Unbreakable as much as I did. I am recommending it as a must read to all of my coaches and all of my friends.

Finally, I want to thank Sifu for creating a book that is touching, sincere and practical. Sifu, thank you for showing us all that no matter how many setbacks, obstacles, or challenges we face, overcoming them only serves to make us stronger and capable of becoming unbreakable.

Berry Fowler
Founder and former Chairman of Sylvan Learning Centers and Founder and Chairman of Fowler International Academy of Professional Coaching and the Fowler School of Business and Executive Coaching

• Introduction •

Introduction

Have you ever felt like you marched to the beat of a different drummer? When I was younger, I was often called a dreamer. It was usually said in a reproachful way, as though by setting my sights on anything above or outside of "the norm," I would be wasting time and energy better spent living according to the expectations of those around me.

Growing up, I can remember a distinct feeling that I was different from my peers. Not better, not worse, just different, as though I did not fit in. I spent a lot of time examining this feeling: Why me? Why do I feel this way? Why can't I just be like everyone else? Why am I being criticized for thinking differently? Is it really such a bad thing?

That feeling made for a lonely existence at times, especially as a child, but the fact that I didn't always relate to other children allowed me to expand my imagination and have deep, searching conversations with myself. I came to believe that I would do something truly meaningful with my life.

Many of you might find it hard to believe, but I am introverted by nature. At various points in my life, I have struggled with my self-confidence. I didn't always have the presence of mind and sense of self that I do now. Strong-willed people are often misunderstood; their ambition and determination can easily be misconstrued. There were times I gave in and tried to become the person the world seemed to expect me to be. It felt good to fit in for a while, but I knew I was pretending and that feeling wouldn't last. God kept calling me to find something greater inside of myself. The journey would most certainly not be easy, but nothing worth doing ever is.

My first love was music. In my family, Friday nights were chore nights. My mom would spring for the latest 45 (that's a single from the latest album, for those of you born in the digital era), and as the whole family cleaned together, we would listen, sing, and dance around to the music of Roberta Flack, The Jackson Five, Kool and the Gang, The Sylvers, and all the others.

I would imagine myself onstage singing in front of thousands of people, all enjoying themselves listening to my songs. Even as that shy, unassuming kid, I wanted to captivate and inspire people with my work, though at that time I had no idea how it would come to pass.

I was in the 3rd grade when I was introduced to the musical *The Man of La Mancha*. I was utterly taken with this movie. In Don Quixote, the perpetual dreamer, I found a character with whom I could connect. He refused to see the bleak reality of things, living on a higher plane and fulfilling his grand dreams, and influencing the people around him to do likewise.

While I did not end up making a career of music, it is still a very big part of my life. I am moved by music and draw motivation and encouragement from it. I even have a song that I associate with each chapter of this book, and wish I could attach a soundtrack so you could experience that form of inspiration as you read. For this introduction, it's "Nothing Comes to Sleepers" by The Gap Band, with its refrain "Oh life is but a dream…nothing comes to sleepers but a dream."

As I grew older and got more and more involved with my martial arts training, it became my primary focus and my passion. I felt that this could be my way to make an impact. I had some major obstacles to overcome in order to achieve my dream of becoming a world champion in Kung Fu, including recovery and retraining after a major car accident.

Through sheer determination and strength of will, I was able to make it happen. I believe that God spared my life for a reason in that car accident. I was entrusted with a second chance to make a difference, and after my brush with death, I was determined to make the most of the opportunity I was given. I wanted to inspire others and show them that they could achieve anything with the right mindset, and with everlasting spirit.

For all of us, there are certain moments that define our lives. Some are happy; some are sad; some are downright frustrating, but they are all part of a perfect plan. These are the moments we hold on to and from which we draw inspiration when we need it most.

God has a calling for each of us and He is preparing us for our destiny. After my car accident, things looked bleak; it seemed as though my dream would die, yet winning the world championship after all I had been through was even more meaningful than I could possibly have imagined, had I not experienced that struggle. Sometimes when you feel like everything is falling to pieces, perhaps all those pieces are actually falling into place.

Searching past outward appearances into the depths of the soul, right into the very presence of God, is what makes someone unbreakable. In life, we go through both positive and negative experiences. In the dark moments, when we are uncertain of how or even if we will overcome our circumstances, we can find God. He can help us see past our limited perception of the situation. It is during the bleakest times when we feel that He has forgotten us, that we will find strength through seeking God and His will for our lives.

We will realize that He has never left us at all, but carried us through when we barely survived. Through our own unyielding spirit and the support of God, we can become unbreakable.

In this book, I have recalled some of the defining moments in my life that have taken me to the next level of my journey. These are but a few; there are many more. They have enabled me to develop my personal philosophy, tap into my courage, and persevere to achieve success beyond my circumstances.

It is my hope that you will be able to identify and access these seminal moments in your own life, and then use them to attain your higher purpose. My goal is for you to be inspired to discover that an indomitable spirit lives inside of you as well, and achieve the state that I call *Unbreakable*.

I will also share some of the stories from my own life, in the hope that they will illustrate my points and inspire you on your own journey. However, it takes action to make change—so I've also included some exercises to help you apply these ideas to your own situation. My clients tell me that these are some of the most beneficial exercises I use in my private coaching practice, so I hope you will use them.

Being *Unbreakable* doesn't mean nothing will ever happen to you, or that you won't have rough patches in your life. There will always be things in life you can't control, some of which can be deeply painful. Becoming *Unbreakable* is about developing the right perspective, being able to recognize when you need to reset, and knowing how to pick yourself up and live again.

To build upon one of my favorite quotes by Dr. Wayne Dyer, I believe we all have a song within us, so "don't die with your music still inside you." Whether it is a song, a book, a poem, or whatever you personally recognize as the most meaningful, find it.

Go beyond the limits of your imagination. Become *Unbreakable*.

• CHAPTER 1 •

The Butterfly Story

A man found a cocoon of a butterfly. One day a small opening appeared; he sat and watched the butterfly for several hours as it struggled to force its body through that little hole. Then it seemed to stop making any progress. It appeared as if it had gotten as far as it could and it could go no farther.

Then the man decided to help the butterfly, so he took a pair of scissors and snipped off the remaining bit of the cocoon. The butterfly then emerged easily. But it had a swollen body and small, shriveled wings.

The man continued to watch the butterfly because he expected that, at any moment, the wings would enlarge and expand to be able to support the body, which would contract in time.

Neither happened! In fact, the butterfly spent the rest of its life crawling around with a swollen body and shriveled wings. It never was able to fly.

What this man in his kindness and haste did not understand was that the restricting cocoon and the struggle required for the butterfly to get through the tiny opening were nature's way of forcing fluid from the body of the butterfly into its wings so that it would be ready for flight once it achieved its freedom from the cocoon."

And such it is within our own lives, our struggles help us to truly soar the great heights of life; struggles in life are necessary.

—Author Unknown

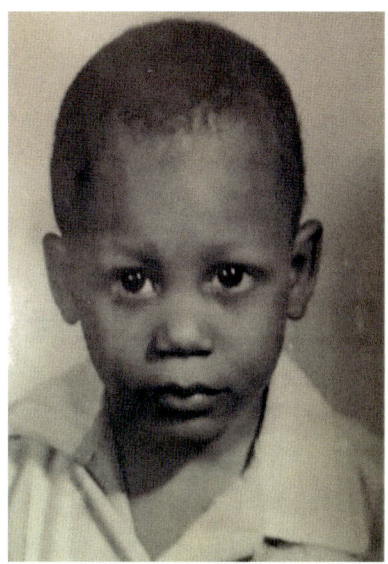

Growth Through Challenge

I was born on September 24, 1967, in Port-au-Prince, Haiti. My parents moved our family to New York. Like so many parents who immigrated to America, my mom and dad were seeking a better life for us. They both worked to support our family. From an early age, they instilled within us the value of education and hard work. I am grateful for the opportunities my parents gave me when they decided to move to the United States.

I originally sought out Kung Fu training for the same reason that thousands of other people around the world began to train in Kung Fu: the influence of a man from Hong Kong named Bruce Lee. Today, I have been studying and training in the martial arts for forty years.

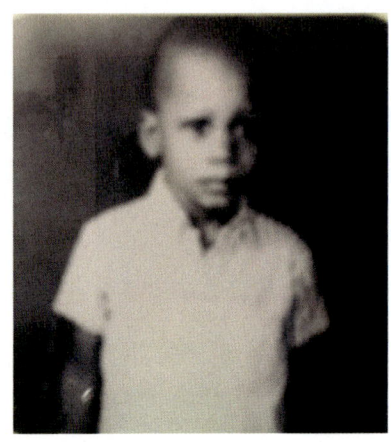

I was ten years old when I found my first Kung Fu instructor, Mr. Reuben Prett, and began training. Upon meeting him, I thought, "I want to be just like him." Mr. Prett guided me in my Kung Fu journey for the next fourteen years—from a novice to a world champion. He encouraged me to train with my eye on the prize of the world championship. He also encouraged me to become an instructor in Kung Fu.

My Kung Fu training was very different than you find in most martial arts academies today. Located in Pearl River, New York, it was not a commercial school. To train there, you had to receive an invitation. The school did not have air conditioning in the summer or heat in the winter. We sparred without any sparring gear. Punches and kicks were real punches and kicks. The workouts lasted two hours, and we went to class three days a week. If it sounds "old school," that's because it was. But I loved it.

I especially loved the philosophical overtones of Mr. Prett's training. He trained his students in the way of the Wu Te—the Martial Virtue. He taught ideals of right and wrong. He expected his students to show respect and to be loyal. He trained his students not to misuse their skills. He taught us more than just the skills of Kung Fu; he taught us how to live life. He taught us how to live the martial way.

Mr. Prett also expected all his students to learn about Chinese culture—ancient China, modern China, the history, the people, the country, the terrain, food, clothing, religion, and philosophy. Training in Kung Fu was a broad education.

In 1985, I attended my first national martial arts tournament in Washington, D.C. Dennis Brown hosted the tournament, and the biggest names in Kung Fu were there: Willie "The Bam" Johnson, Keith Hirabayashi, Richard Branden, and Cynthia Rothrock. At this tournament, I caught the fever to compete. Five years later, I would be world champion.

After graduating from high school in 1986, I traveled to California to train. While in California, I trained with Eric Chen and Keith Hirabayashi. After three weeks, I came back to New York and took different jobs so that I could buy a car and pay the bills. As I was doing this, I continued to focus on tournament training. I got ranked in the top 25 in the PKL (Professional Karate League) regional rankings.

I was on my way, and the future was bright.

Then, on April 13, 1988, I was driving across the Tappan Zee bridge on my way to work. I was cut off by another driver and lost control of my car causing me to spin out across two lanes and hit the divider. I was hurt badly, but my seatbelt saved my life.

Unfortunately, the accident left me with a severely injured back. The doctors told me that I had misaligned vertebrae in my spine. They added, "It is not likely that you will be able to practice the martial arts again."

As you can imagine, I was devastated.

For a while, I accepted my fate. I went to tournaments and watched and observed others—people I had beaten prior to the accident—winning. I thought to myself, "That should be me." I drifted and became lost and confused, quite uncertain about my future. I could have died in that accident, but God spared my life. I knew I could not just give up.

This would be my first major *reset*.

One night, after speaking with a close friend who encouraged me to return to competition, I made up my mind; I *would* return.

To begin the journey to my comeback, I began to train with fellow martial artist and competitor, Richard Branden in his hometown of Lynn, Massachusetts. There, we shared many experiences and trained hard together. Richie's life story has been influential and very meaningful to me, the inspiration behind many of my own accomplishments. He had overcome many challenges in his life, one of which was being blind in one eye. Because he never let anything stop him, he became one of the best competitors of my generation.

Richie also loved music. I remember the first time I pulled up to his school. I didn't know if it was a dance club or martial arts academy. He would crank the tunes as we trained; the louder the music, the harder he pushed us. In training with Richie, I added extra components such as weight training, running, visualization, and a very intense stretching routine.

Richie went on to become the "Yin/Yang Man" in a television show called "WMAC Masters," and the Black Power Ranger on the TV show the "Power Rangers".

In 1990, I represented the United States in international competition at the World Association of Kickboxing Organizations' World Championship, in Venice, Italy. There, I accomplished a dream that many thought was impossible.

I became a world champion.

All my training had paid off. There were many lessons I learned from this experience. I learned about pain, suffering, and choices.

> *Suffering produces perseverance; perseverance produces character; and character produces hope.*
>
> *– Romans 5:2b-4 MSG*

I learned that while pain in life is inevitable, *suffering* is optional. Suffering is a choice: we may be in physical or mental pain, but we can either choose to do something about it, or just wallow in it and endure it.

Master your pain, to break through it with perseverance. Perseverance is the quality that will allow you to continue trying, despite difficulties or obstacles, when battling insurmountable odds—when the feeling of discouragement is about to overtake you. Perseverence is holding steadfast to your dreams until God comes through and answers your prayers.

Times of challenge are when your true character can be developed. They let you prepare for something in the future, like building the muscles you need to have hope, to know that you can overcome, and that brighter days are still ahead.

During dark and difficult times, you must have hope; you must maintain a crystal-clear vision of where you are going, and what you want. In the introduction, I spoke of how, as a child, I felt a connection with Don Quixote, the hero in *Man of La Mancha*. I find the song "The Impossible Dream" from that same production to be powerfully inspiring. It has been recorded by numerous big names and I wouldn't even try to guess how many school graduation ceremonies it has been played at. The song is familiar to us all, with its lyrics "to fight the unbeatable foe," and "to bear with unbearable sorrow." It expresses the indomitable spirit I want to help you grow.

Having hope will help you trust the process, because we are always in the process. The moments of victory are but seconds; the process can be months, years, decades and you can't stop, you must keep pushing through. You must fall in love with the process to become *Unbreakable!*

• CHAPTER 2 •

The Secret Of Success

I am going to tell you a little story about a man who wanted to know the secret of success, and decided to find out from a Guru.

Now, this Guru was a wise old sage who knew every secret of Life. He lived in splendid isolation on a mountain-top. Our hero set out on his difficult journey to meet this wise man.

He was determined to reach the top, and so he overcame many obstacles on his way. Fighting through thick forests, scaling huge boulders, and escaping from wild beasts, at last, he clambered to the peak and lay on the ground, gasping for breath.

A few minutes later, he sat up... and beheld the Guru seated in deep meditation.

Silently, he waited. Almost an hour later, the Guru opened his eyes and glanced at the man. He raised an inquiring eyebrow.

The man stammered, "Oh wise and all-knowing seer, I come to you in search of the secret of success."

The Guru didn't reply. He simply stood up and started walking down the hill.

The man followed. He found it difficult to keep pace with the old man, who seemed to skip from one rock to the other like a mountain-goat. They walked steadily for another hour, and he wondered if they were going back to the foothills.

Suddenly, they came upon a clearing. In the middle was a clear lake. The waters were still, glinting softly in the rays of a setting sun.

The Guru walked up to the edge of the lake and beckoned the man closer. With a gesture, he asked him to kneel down.

Unquestioningly, the man did as the Guru ordered.

Suddenly, he felt himself seized by a strong hand at the back of his neck. His head was forced down under the water, and held there firmly.

"This is some kind of test," said the man to himself, as he sat still.

A minute passed, and he was growing breathless. The grip on his neck hadn't weakened. Another minute crawled by, and now he was getting anxious. His heart beat heavily in his chest, his throat tightened, and his lungs screamed for air.

He struggled to arise, and the old man's grip became even stronger, pressed him further down into the water.

Now, the man was in a panic. He thrashed around wildly, trying with all his energy to loosen the vise around his neck. Precious seconds passed, and he felt his strength slowly ebbing away.

He thought he was going to die!

Just as he was about to give up hope, ruing his folly in ever coming here, the hand on his collar let go.

Violently leaping onto the shore, the man drew in his breath in heaving gasps. Delicious oxygen flooded his lungs. His vision grew clearer, the hammering in his throat slowed down, his hands stopped trembling.

And he felt a deep anger welling up from within himself.

Standing up, he faced the Guru and screamed: "Are you CRAZY? You could have killed me!"

The Guru simply stared at him for a long moment.

Then he spoke for the first time.

"You wanted to know the secret of success. Here it is. Do you remember, just a few minutes ago, how badly you wanted to take that next breath of air? **When you want success that badly, you will have it. That is the secret of success."**

Without saying another word, he turned around and walked back to his hilltop abode.

—Author unknown

What is the number one quality you must have in order to be successful? You must **desire** it at the level needed in order to succeed. Desire is simply a strong feeling of wanting to have something.

Think about your childhood. Children apply this principle quite well. Think about it, when a child truly desires something, they are relentless. They will not stop asking until they get what they want. They don't focus on the possibility that it may not happen. We need to approach our goals with the same mindset—a childlike faith.

The Story of My Success

In late 2001, my wife at the time was in medical school and pregnant with our daughter, Hope. I was running a martial arts academy in Nyack, New York. We were getting by and I was happy to have a great career doing what I love to do.

When I found out we were having a child I realized I needed to do better financially. I had been in my martial arts business for a while and had worked with several consultants. I had heard about people doing well financially in my industry so I knew it was possible for me, but I could not figure out the details to make it happen.

I had always believed if you seek you shall find. So, I went on a journey to discover the secret of transforming my business and financial life.

During my quest, I heard a famous martial arts business expert speak about his system. I remember thinking that everything he is saying makes sense. So, I started calling around and was told I need to speak with his head trainer.

The first day I spoke with him, I was very impressed with his knowledge. He had a way of speaking that very clearly defined the student/mentor relationship he would like to forge.

I fought against his ideas and suggestions for about two weeks. Then I realized the definition of insanity is doing the same thing repeatedly and expecting a different result. No one had talked to me about the martial arts business that way before. I still thought his ideas would never work, yet I decided to give it a shot.

As soon as I did, everything changed. In the first few weeks, I literally doubled my gross revenues. By the third month, I had exceeded my expectations by

$10,000. So, what was it that had changed? My location? My school? My students? No...what had changed was me—my outlook, combined with systems to support it. He had shifted my beliefs and took me to a place that I had only dreamed of financially.

In a ten-month period, I had more than quadrupled my income, and within 18 months I went from one location to three. At that point, I went to work for him as one of his top consultants, teaching and sharing the information I had learned. Again, this was another growth period for me, as now I had to lead by example with my own academies and help my group of mentoring clients duplicate my results.

I learned many concepts from this experience, I understood how and why we need to constantly educate ourselves differently to move forward. It's not always education in the traditional sense. But it is about learning, reimagining, reinventing our idea who we think we are and what we are doing.

We need to be open to the idea of reinventing ourselves. It is not just about change—change can be temporary since we can always go back. As I said before when we reinvent, we transform, we become a new thing.

No one is perfect, and no one knows everything there is to know. Thankfully, we don't need to know everything, but we do need to recognize when we need to learn something new, and when we need to develop our skills and abilities. Ask yourself:

    1. How can I tell it's time to change?

    2. What are the steps I need to take right now?

    3. How can I let go and be more accepting of my circumstance?

4. How can I rise above it?

Generally speaking, this will help you have the right sort of attitude. For example, it's best not to get too worried about what it is you cannot do. When we worry, we are focusing on something that has not happened yet, we are future focused.

> *"Yesterday is history. Tomorrow is a mystery. Today is a gift—that's why it's called the present."*
>
> —George Bernard Shaw

Rather, we should take the knowledge of our shortcomings and examine ways in which we can improve. Worrying will do you no good. Our energy should be directed towards working on what it is we need to do better and how to accomplish it. As my mentor, Fred Mertens, used to say, "Don't let what you can do affect what you will do".

> *"Worry does not empty tomorrow of its sorrow. It empties today of its strength."*
>
> – Corrie Ten Boom

Therefore I tell you, do not worry about your life, what you will eat or drink; or about your body, what you will wear. Is not life more than food, and the body more than clothes? Look at the birds of the air; they do not sow or reap or store away in barns, and yet your heavenly Father feeds them. Are you not much more valuable than they? Can any one of you by worrying add a single hour to your life?

—Matthew 6:25-27 MSG

[Place Your Life Before God] So here's what I want you to do, God helping you: Take your everyday, ordinary life—your sleeping, eating, going-to-work, and walking-around life—and place it before God as an offering. Embracing what God does for you is the best thing you can do for him. Don't become so well-adjusted to your culture that you fit into it without even thinking. Instead, fix your attention on God. You'll be transformed from the inside out. Readily recognize what he wants from you, and quickly respond to it. Unlike the culture around you, always dragging you down to its level of immaturity, God brings the best out of you, develops well-formed maturity in you.

—Romans 12:2 MSG

So, the question is how do we transform? How do we go beyond who we think we are to, what we can become, from the caterpillar to the butterfly? I can remember asking myself this question so many times, just feeling like who I am, what I am doing, who I am being, is not working.

One day, I was speaking to an associate while I was going through a very difficult time. She looked at me and gave me the best advice I was ever given—reinvent yourself! She reminded me of my past success, explained that I already possessed the formula for success, that if I could do it once I could do it again. With that, I was off and running. It gave me the confidence to let go and move forward in a very new way - a way I had not considered.

I began to ask myself a different question: who do I choose to become now? It was the beginning of a new chapter in my life. A sense of transformation started to occur with each step I took in this new direction, I felt empowered and I felt a deeper sense of confidence.

Confidence is everything, and confidence in your ability to learn and improve will make an amazing difference to your success. If you are convinced that you cannot learn something, then you have already lost the battle. If you can tell yourself, "what one person can do, so can another," this is a sign that you are on the way to success.

The poem *Thinking* was published in 1905 and has often been printed with slight alterations, and without credit to its author. The original version is below, but I learned it as *The Winner's Creed*, and used to recite it repeatedly to develop a deeper sense of confidence. Try reading it aloud now, and notice how you feel.

Thinking

If you think you are beaten, you are
If you think you dare not, you don't,
If you like to win, but you think you can't
It is almost certain you won't.

If you think you'll lose, you're lost
For out of the world we find,
Success begins with a fellow's will
It's all in the state of mind.

If you think you're outclassed, you are
You've got to think high to rise,
You've got to be sure of yourself before
You can ever win a prize.

Life's battles don't always go
To the stronger or faster man,
But sooner or later the man who wins
Is the man WHO THINKS HE CAN!
                              —Walter D. Wintle

Developing Self-Confidence

I'm passionate about the importance of self-confidence. I would not have achieved all that I have if I hadn't realized my need to develop my own self-confidence. As I explained earlier, I came to a point in my life when I realized my motivation and belief that I could become a World Champion had to come from within.

I decided to build my own belief in my ability to achieve this goal, and I had to commit to renewing this belief on a daily basis. In short, I had to develop a deep and abiding self-confidence and be deliberate about growing it daily. What I learned along the way was life changing.

Self-confidence is what separates the average from the expert, the mediocre from the extraordinary. You can have great talent, but without the belief that you can achieve that goal, that talent will be wasted. You won't have the heart to keep going, to overcome setbacks, obstacles, or defeats.

As an athlete, your confidence is in a state of continual flux, as if you are on a road that has curves and continual ups and downs. I believe the reason why is because athletes are constantly striving to do better, to be better, since they are judged on how well they perform whether in practice or during game time.

I remember a conversation I had with a pro athlete where he said, "There is no other job in the world like it. We cannot have a bad day, we must always do our best because there is always another person trying his best to take your job." This is a very powerful and true statement.

People from all walks of life can experience a dip in their confidence and relate to this experience in their own way. Our confidence might dip because of something someone said or we might have had some experience that we are beating ourselves up for. The latter is most likely the greatest reason for all people to suffer a dip in confidence levels.

Think of it like this: When you are driving your car, you have a big windshield in front of you, and you also have a rear-view mirror, but it is a lot smaller because you can't drive forward while looking back. If you do, eventually you will crash. The rear-view mirrors in our life serve a purpose, of course. They can remind us of the lessons we have learned.

However, if we spend too much time looking back and beating ourselves up it will no longer serve us. Instead of being a reminder of lessons, it will become a reason for our failure; a reason why we aren't good enough.

Self-confidence is extremely important. It will influence how other people see you, and how much others trust you both as an individual, and as a part of a team. If you can put aside self-doubt and mistrust, and stop thinking that you "can't do this" or "can't do that," you are on your way to increasing self-confidence and success.

Some people are born with mounds of self-confidence; for others, however, it is something that needs to be worked on as we mature. This is because many of us have been told that we are useless, incapable, not good enough, and that we will never win etc. There may have been unfortunate experiences with family members or perhaps there was bullying at school or by others in the neighborhood.

Whatever the cause, it is important to unlearn those views of yourself, even when they have been internalized over many years. It is always worth letting go of self-doubt and re-learning about your own self-worth.

We have something inside us all that makes us want to challenge the boundaries of our imagination. Think about it—throughout history, we have challenged the status quo. We learned the world is round, not flat, we have gone to the moon, created light, and cellphones. We can send a signal anywhere in the world so we can communicate and see each other in real time.

When we challenge the boundaries of our imagination we grow in our self-worth and confidence. We discover purpose, passion and we begin to see and experience what we are made of. Even if you were told you were not good enough, you couldn't make it, or were bullied, there remains inside you this gift of imagination.

Allow yourself to stretch it, listen to your heart and not the naysayers and dream killers. You can rise above your circumstance and find the champion within you. What barriers will you break? I know this is easier said than done. How can we achieve this? How can we stretch beyond our perceived limitations?

There are lots of ways that you can achieve this. Self-hypnosis, using affirmations and role-playing techniques are all possible aids in learning to develop self-confidence.

For all of these methods, you will need to understand that we are programmed. Our brain, our conscious and subconscious minds, operate like a computer. If we pile into the brain statements about how worthless, unproductive and lousy we are, then the brain will fill our data bank with this information and program it accordingly.

When we ensure that our brain is told that we are able, can learn, and can achieve, that we are champions and have a bright future ahead of us, then our data bank will be programmed with this and we will create a life that reflects this.

One of the most powerful exercises I do with my coaching clients is called the belief exercise. Our beliefs are formed from ideas that we allow to take root. Once an idea takes root it impacts what we create in our lives and how we see the world. It becomes our filter. It colors how we see the world.

For example, if we were to put on brown tinted sunglasses we would see the world as brown. If we were to put on sunglasses with blue tint we would see the world as blue. Now, if we put on clear glasses then things would appear clear, no color or tint. This is a large part of how we are programmed. We have beliefs that are indoctrinated that create our view point of the world, they color or tint our view. Do you ever stop to consider what you believe and how that is impacting your view of the world? How are your beliefs impacting the situations in your life? Do you recognize that you are responsible for what you are creating in your life?

Try the belief exercise yourself.

Belief Exercise

Step 1: Write down the first thing that comes to mind as you answer the following.

3 things you believe about:

    Yourself

    Relationships

    Work

    Money

    The future

Step 2: Go through each answer you wrote, write down your level of certainty about the belief, and place a number next to each answer using this scale:

1 = absolute | 2 = not sure | 3 = not at all

Step 3: You need to decide whether or not the belief is helpful or impeding; again, go through each of your answers. If the belief is helpful, put an (H) next to your answer. If the answer is impeding put (IMP).

Step 4: For the last step, decide whether or not the belief is deliberately chosen or indoctrinated. If it is deliberate, write the letters (DEL) next to your answer, or if it is indoctrinated, write the letters (IND).

Then go back and review each step. What is present for you? What do you recognize? How are your beliefs impacting your life?

Working With Your Subconscious

Opening the channel to the subconscious is the key to internalizing the positive data. Try playing an audio recording of affirmations when you are just about to go to sleep. When you are in a sleep mode, your subconscious is much more open to suggestion. So, your conscious mind switches off, and your subconscious mind is receptive to the affirmations you hear.

Lay on your bed, shut your eyes, place one hand over your belly, feel your breath as your belly rises and falls. Place your other hand over your heart, feel your heart beating as you lay there. Allow the words of the recording to penetrate your mind, body, and soul. Your subconscious mind will accept the information and any instructions it receives. This positive message will help you convince yourself that you are strong, capable, and confident, as if hypnotizing one's self.

Self-hypnosis is really about learning how to open the door to your subconscious mind, and to input the information that you want – in a similar way that someone else, like a professional hypnotist, would do. There are many ways to harness the power of self-hypnosis. Using audio recordings is a good way of deliberately receiving the information you want.

"Repeating affirmations" is another effective technique and can be done anywhere and at any time. Here is an example of how to incorporate affirmations into your life

First thing in the morning, while you are getting ready in the bathroom, look at yourself in the mirror and repeat your affirmations. For example:

- I am a confident and capable person. I am an achiever.
- I am successful. I work hard and deserve to succeed.

- I find solutions when there are challenges. Everything always works out for me.
- I am goal oriented and focused. I will succeed.

Add 3 of your own affirmations:

1._____

2._____

3._____

For affirmations to be effective, they must be repeated on a regular basis, with emotion and belief in what you are saying. This way it will influence your mind and thus your thoughts.

The mind always wants to be right, if this is true we need to consider the result of our thinking. For example, if you are guilty of negative thinking, what kind of actions are you taking? What kind of results are you getting? Now let us look at the opposite. If you think about any situation in a positive manner you are more likely to get a positive result.

If we then ask ourselves, "What sort of person am I?" it is the data in the brain that will give us the answer. So, a data bank full of positive information will give positive answers.

Here is a true story that shows what I mean. My co-host Jacqui and I were in a parking garage and when we went in we did not realize we needed a ticket. So, on the way out the guard stopped us and asked why we didn't have a ticket. I explained what happened in a calm voice. The guard walked away and said she was calling her supervisor.

When she did that I turned to Jacqui and said, "I have the favor of God and everything always works out for me." Now it had been a long and tiring day. She looked over at me and I could not tell what she was thinking, but I told her, "Just wait, you will see." So, the supervisor came, asked us what happened and sent us on our way with no fee, no hassle, nothing. This is a prime example of how self-confidence and positive thoughts can impact a situation.

Self-confidence is the key to learning new skills and, progressing in your work and home life. It is the foundation of all self-development. Self-confidence allows you to deal with life's challenges effectively. When someone knows what to do, they naturally feel confident in their ability to handle difficult situations.

Another technique to develop confidence is to role play through potential situations. Athletes develop skill through practice and repetition, the same can be true with confidence.

Observe a child learning to walk. They keep trying even though they fall. We encourage them to keep trying, and after many attempts they accomplish it. They begin to walk and eventually run. They attain the skill through practice and repetition.

When we role play, we gain valuable practice and repetition of how to act in each situation. This will help us to feel confident. Take a basic situation like having a conversation with a new client, potential mate, friend or job interview. Pick a trusted friend to help you, let them play the role of the other person, and work through all the potential responses they might have.

Remember when you are role playing to act as if it is real. Pay attention to your breath, posture and body language. This will help you to prepare, and to feel more comfortable and confident.

> *"It is official: New Horizons has survived its close flyby of the Pluto system unscathed. 'We have a healthy spacecraft, we have a healthy system, and we are outbound for Pluto,' Alice Bowman, mission operations manager for New Horizons, said... 'It was just like we practiced...'"*
>
> *—As reported in the Los Angeles Times July 14, 2015*

• CHAPTER 3 •

6 Principles To RESET And Become *Unbreakable*

A "RESET" is about starting afresh. When I talk about re-setting your life, it is a chance to start again with a fresh slate, an opportunity to create new possibilities for yourself. Just like a computer, I believe people need to reboot or reset themselves every so often in order to run smoothly. If you look up the definition of the word reset, it means "to move (something) back to an original place" thus my explanation of starting over from the beginning.

An alternate definition is "to put something back in the correct place for healing." Typically, this meaning is understood to refer specifically to fixing a broken bone, however, I find it relevant and significant in our interpretation of the word as well.

In my life, I have RESET many times; overcoming the injuries from my car accident to become a Martial Arts World Champion, transitioning from an athlete to a business person, becoming a father, going through a divorce, and launching my life coaching business.

One of the things I have come to understand is that resetting is necessary, and the result will make you a more resilient person. Resetting will take faith and courage. I have learned both these lessons personally, through my martial arts and my walk with God.

Resiliency is about being able to recoil or spring back. It is the ability to recover from or adjust easily to misfortune or change, such as illness, depression, or any adversity we might face. In short, it is about becoming unbreakable. One of the best suggestions I received, while going through a difficult time in my life, was to make myself resilient by resetting and reinventing myself.

When I speak of the idea of reinventing oneself, it is not merely about changing your situation. Change is temporary; we can always go back to the way things were if it doesn't work out. When we reinvent ourselves, we transform; we become something new.

> *"Therefore, if anyone is in Christ, he is a new creature; the old things passed away; behold, new things have come"*
> *– 2 Corinthians 5:17 MSG*

> *"And do not be conformed to this world, but be transformed by the renewing of your mind"*
> —Romans 12:2

So the question is, how do we transform?

> *"You must be shapeless, formless, like water. When you pour water in a cup, it becomes the cup. When you pour water in a bottle, it becomes the bottle. When you pour water in a teapot, it becomes the teapot. Water can drip and it can crash. Become like water my friend."*
> —Bruce Lee

Take a look at your own life. How many times have you needed to reset? Are you aware of the times when you were in need of a reset but did not follow through? Will you be able to identify the moments in your life which call for a reset?

In this chapter I will lay out the steps and tools I believe are necessary to facilitate not just a recovery, but a transformation. There are six principles to conquer on your path to living your life with maximum resiliency, by becoming Unbreakable - the ultimate reset.

RESET Principle #1 – Truth

In order to RESET and become unbreakable, you must be truthful with yourself, specifically about the areas in your life that need a RESET, and why. If there are many areas you need to RESET, start with the one that will empower you the most, so that you can attack all the other areas with the vigor and enthusiasm necessary to be victorious!

> *The truth will set you free.*
> —John 8:32 MSG

It is a fact. The truth does set you free. It frees you from living a life that is not authentic to who you are. Think about it: when were you the happiest and most fulfilled? When have you felt the most disconnected? Do you notice how these feelings align with whether you are living truthfully?

I believe most of our struggles in life come from not living our truth. It is not uncommon to make decisions in our lives based on other people's desires. We can end up choosing even something as important as a career or relationship simply because we are trying to make someone else happy. That's not to say there is anything wrong with wanting to please other people, but it is vital that we stay faithful to our own purpose as well. We each have our own authentic purpose in life; we must do our best to live it.

"Always be yourself, express yourself, have faith in yourself. Do not go out and look for a successful personality and duplicate him."
—*Bruce Lee*

Being able to honestly express yourself, to get in touch with your inner voice and understand the truth you are seeking, is essential to discovering your heart essence. What is your heart essence? It is the silent voice that we hear when our mind is quieted. It is the voice of God. There is nothing more calming, more serene, or more honest than that quiet voice. Like God, it is within us. There is only one thing that can get in the way of that voice, and that is the ego.

The ego can be quite powerful. It feeds on fear, insecurity, past hurt or pain, competitiveness or dominance, protective behavior, and keeps us from the truth and growth that we are in touch with when we are living in our essence. In order to overcome the ego, we have to learn to work with our essence.

As my good friend Karen Hoyos, a renowned life coach, speaker, and best-selling author explains the subject, in order to overcome the ego, we have to learn to work with our essence. Overcoming the ego is the key. But, what exactly is ego? Simply put, the ego is...

E - Edging
G - God
O - Out

It takes practice to overcome the ego. I will share with you a powerful tool.

If you utilize this tool, it could make the difference in whether you are operating in ego or heart essence. This tool is called: I Should, I Would, I Could, and its use begins with examining the Circle of Individual Perspective.

> *Remember, knowing is not enough. We must apply.*
> *—Bruce Lee*

Circle of Individual Perspective

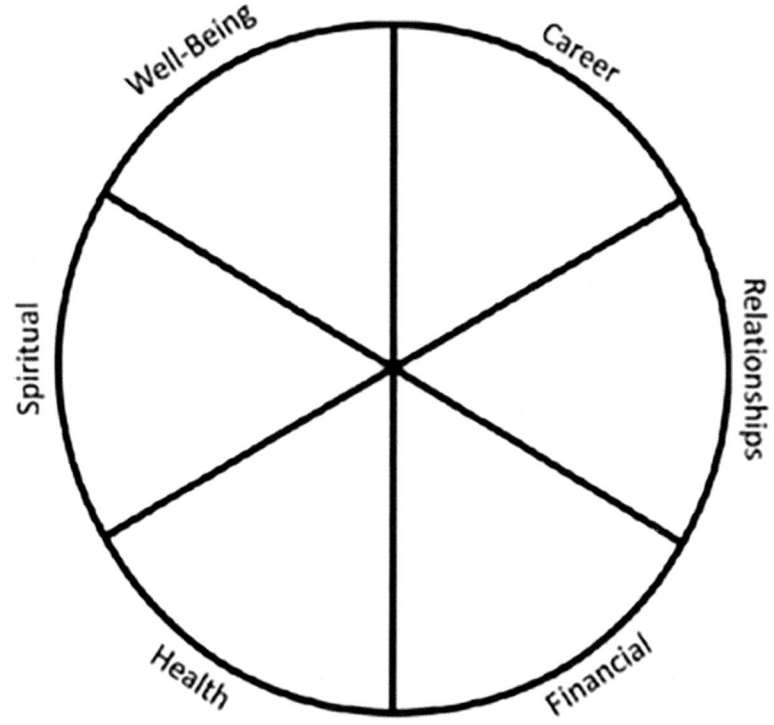

Illustration courtesy of Berry Fowler,
Fowler International Academy of Professional Coaching

To do this exercise, consider each of these six areas of your life and give each area a score from 1-10, with 1 being that it is not going well at all, and 10 meaning it is so good it can't get any better.

Any area lower than a 7 is an area of concern, and we will address these in the following exercise.

I Should, I Would, I Could Exercise

Please complete the following sentences. Based on an area that scored low on the Circle of Individual Perspective...

1. I should_____.

2. I should_____.

3. I should_____.

4. I should_____.

5. I should_____.

1. I should, because_____.

2. I should, because_____.

3. I should, because_____.

4. I should, because_____.

5. I should, because_____.

The Truth Behind Would

Now take your answers to the "should" section and consider this. If anything were possible, I would:

1. I would_____.

2. I would_____.

3. I would_____.

4. I would_____.

5. I would_____.

Now add on to those answers by completing the following sentences.

1. I would, but_____.

2. I would, but_____.

3. I would, but_____.

4. I would, but_____.

5. I would, but_____.

What does the word "would" mean? It is a verb that is equal to the past of will. It expresses a condition, indicating the consequences of an imagined event or situation. Take a look at your answers. What are your conditions? Are they real or imagined?

Please complete the following sentences. What could you choose?

1. If I really wanted to, I could_____.

2. If I really wanted to, I could_____.

3. If I really wanted to, I could_____.

4. If I really wanted to, I could_____.

5. If I really wanted to, I could_____.

Truth: Why haven't you?

1. I could, but_____.

2. I could, but_____.

3. I could, but_____.

4. I could, but_____.

5. I could, but_____.

What did you notice about your answers? What is the truth?

_____

_____

_____

Recognizing the truth is the first step to transformation.

Should

We spend a lot of time learning or being pushed to compensate for expectation or obligation. Oftentimes we begin to create a list of things that we should do. We should do this or that based on a variety of factors. It is important that we are honest with ourselves about what kind of *shoulds* we hold. More importantly, we must assess the things we consider to be *shoulds* and check them against what is right for us. Sometimes those objectives are not in alignment with the current goals that we have. Monitor and adjust your *shoulds* in order to relieve unnecessary stress.

Would

The word "would" is the past of will. It is also conditional. The reasons items on our *woulds* list never get done are usually similar to why our should list is neglected.

There is a great line in the movie *At Sachem Farm,* in which Nigel Hawthorne, playing the kooky old uncle, asks his nephew, "Have you ever considered that the reason the things you do don't work out is because you continue to do things that aren't meant for you?" When there are conditions for success, you must decide honestly if those conditions can be overcome. Those who place their attention on the things that come naturally to them are accordingly more successful.

Could

Could is the past tense of can. It is used to indicate possibility! The answers to your "I could" exercise should really be thought of as "I can." Your *coulds* operate within your natural and learned skills, therefore you are fully capable of achieving them, provided you get control over the ego.

Claim the truth and decide what you can and shall do in this moment.

In this moment, I_____.

In this moment, I_____.

In this moment, I_____.

In this moment, I_____.

RESET Principle #2 – Thoughts

Do not underestimate your thoughts. They are a crucial part of the RESET process. Whatever you think or believe takes root and will eventually grow to become your reality. Change your thoughts and you change your life! Learn this immediately and you will be successful in mastering your RESET to become *Unbreakable*.

Remember, every action begins with a thought. Thoughts are the seeds, watered by our imagination, that manifest into our destiny. It has been proven that our thoughts help us to focus our attention; we stretch towards the dominating thought of our mind. What are the dominating thoughts of your mind? There is a saying that goes "Watch your thoughts, they become your words. Watch your words, they become your actions. Watch your actions, they become your destiny." We have the ability to create. The question is, are your creating your life deliberately, or is your life happening to you, outside of your control?

We must be wary of what we allow to take root in our minds. We water our thoughts with the words we use, and the thoughts germinate and grow into actions (or inaction). There is also power in the words we allow others to speak for us. Accepting negative words spoken over our lives can have the same effect as though we had spoken them ourselves.

> *The swiftest horse cannot overtake the word once spoken.*
> —*Chinese proverb*

In Chinese medicine, it is believed that the heart and the mind are connected.

> *From the wellspring of the heart, the mouth speaks.*
> —*Matthew 12:34 MSG*

Your mind is like a computer; what you allow in will affect your programing. Once your heart accepts an external, be it positive or negative, it becomes a thought in your mind. Then notice, does that thought influence what you will say? Do you start to speak differently because you are thinking differently? Are you aware of what you are speaking into existence?

> *Above all else, guard your heart, for everything you do flows from it.*
> —*Proverbs 4:23 NIV*

RESET Principle #3 – Purpose

Everyone has a purpose in life! I mentioned this briefly in section number one, about being truthful to yourself. I find that if you are living truthfully, you are most likely living according to your authentic purpose. How about the rest of us who are not quite sure of our purpose, nor how to find it? Let your passions lead you! Your passion will allow your RESET to propel you into your life's purpose.

Finding your life purpose can radically alter the course of your life, for the better. You will feel more focused, motivated, and fulfilled once you are on the path to living your purpose. In addition, knowing your purpose can help you get through the toughest moments when you most need to be *Unbreakable*. Life can sometimes be filled with moments of great emotional pain. Pain, however difficult, can be an opportunity for new growth if you know which direction you are heading.

Answer the following questions to gain a clearer understanding of your life purpose.

Have I been living my life purpose? If not, why?

_____

_____

What advantages would I enjoy if I knew the purpose of my life?

_____

_____

If I am hesitant to find my life purpose, why is that?

_____

_____

Have I located at least three guided meditations on finding my life purpose?

Yes _____/ No _____

What is my end goal? How will things be when I live my life purpose continually?

_____

_____

What steps can I take each day to move toward realizing my vision?

_____

_____

If necessary, how can I monetize my life purpose?

_____

_____

If you are not yet sure of your life purpose, here are some simple questions to help you in your discovery:

- What was your life like growing up? Do a time line of the major events of your life.
- What have you done for the last 10 years? What skills have you developed from your experiences?
- What are your strengths?
- What topics are you most passionate about?
- What do you find yourself talking about most of the time?
- What did you want to do when you were twelve or fourteen?
- If you had all the time and money in the world, what would you do?
- If you only had a year to live, how would you spend it?
- How do you want others to remember you?
- How can you best serve the world?

- What do you dream of doing but are too afraid to try?

Lastly, fill in the blanks of this sentence.

"I help people to _____, so they can _____."

If you take your time and consider your answers to this exercise carefully, it should help you in your search for your life purpose. The answer is inside of you, if you know the right questions to ask yourself.

RESET Principle #4 – Choice

Being mindful of your choices will allow you to create the life you want, and your best future, day by day. You must remain thoughtfully aware of what is best for you, in alignment with your overall purpose, truth, and thoughts. Your decisions matter, so choose carefully and deliberately. Choose YOU because YOU matter and YOU deserve to achieve your goals—and to become *Unbreakable*!

Prefer vs. Afford: We can justify dismissing what we prefer, as long as we convince ourselves that there is a reason we cannot have it. When we do that, we settle for something other than our goal, and sometimes we allow ourselves to forget what it was that we actually wanted in the first place.

Here are some questions to help you evaluate your choices, both in the past and in the future, moving forward.

What are some choices in your life that took you in the wrong direction?

1. _____

2. _____

3. _____

What are some choices in your life that took you in the right direction?

1. _____

2. _____

3. _____

What caused you to make those choices, Ego or Essence?

1. _____

2. _____

3. _____

How will you make choices in the future?

_____

Why?

_____

Do you trust your intuition? Can you make decisions without overthinking them?

Yes / No

What are three important choices you need to make in your life... right now?

1. _____

2. _____

3. _____

One very important aspect of choice is forgiveness. Whether it is on behalf of someone you feel has wronged you, or if it is directed towards your own self, forgiveness always is a choice, and it is up to you to consciously make that choice.

Guilt, shame, and resentment are emotional states that can bring us down. When we feel these emotions, it can feel as if we are carrying around heavy weights. They can cause us to feel a lack of love for ourselves, unworthiness, or even depression. These feelings can be caused by our interpretation of events in our lives. Through true forgiveness of ourselves and others, we can learn to release these feelings and move forward in our lives.

Let's start with looking at guilt. When we are experiencing feelings of guilt, we reinforce the idea that there is something wrong with us. We can lose our sense of self-confidence and self-respect. The key to overcoming feelings of guilt is to recognize that we go through life doing the very best we can with the knowledge and understanding that we possess at any given time.

Making mistakes is part of life. It is how we learn, grow, and understand more about life. We gain wisdom from our experiences. In fact, you have to make mistakes in order to be corrected. For that reason, we should never regret or fear making mistakes. Many times I have heard people express the thought, "If I could only go back, knowing what I know now, I would do something differently," but the truth is if you could go back with more knowledge, how would you have gained the understanding you have today? Instead of immersing ourselves in regret and guilt, we need to embrace these experiences to truly appreciate the lessons we have learned.

> *Forgetting those things which are behind and reaching forward to those things which are ahead, I press toward the goal for the prize.*
> *—Philippians 3:13-14 NKJV*

We need to remember that our mistakes are not us. Sometimes when we make mistakes, we feel like we are being judged negatively, and this can lead to a feeling of shame. Feelings of shame can make us want to hide or withdraw from the source of judgement or from others who we are worried will judge us. Sometimes shame can show itself in someone's appearance. Your choice of what you wear, how you carry yourself, and the words you speak, will reflect your inner world.

> *Shame is a soul eating emotion.* – C.G. Jung

When you resent someone, you hold onto your belief that the person has tried to hurt you, or has made you feel as though you are not worthy. You deny any responsibility for what has occurred. However, you must acknowledge that it takes two people to have a fight. Hopefully, there is at least one person who decides to take the high road and attempt to heal the situation.

Finding your life purpose can radically alter the course of your life, for the better. You will feel more focused, motivated, and fulfilled once you are on the path to living your purpose. Admittedly, there are some situations that may not ever fully heal, but if you made an honest attempt and can find a place in your heart to forgive, I believe that will help you to move forward and not get mired in resentment. When you have feelings of resentment, you become bitter and unable to express love. Resentment can cause you to be overly cautious and guarded, and to make your own life more challenging.

> *Resentment is like drinking poison and waiting for the other person to die.* - St. Augustine (ca 400 AD)

So here is my question to you: Are you willing to forgive yourself? Are you willing to forgive others who have hurt you? Are you willing to look at the facts and understand that people who are hurting pass along their hurt to others? What would happen if you chose to have that perspective? Letting go of hurt, guilt, shame, and resentment is not only for your benefit, but for the benefit of all the people currently in your life. Letting go can only improve your ability to connect with them, and feel whole.

Forgiveness Exercise

Releasing memories of mistakes made, people that you have hurt, and things that you wish you had not done.

Part 1 - Take a few quiet minutes and review your life. If you have been judging or upset with another person for something, get a sheet of paper and on the front side write down everything you are upset or angry with the person about, in this format:

"I forgive _____(person's name) for _____."

When your list is complete, turn the paper over and if there is anything for which you have judged yourself, write it down.

"I forgive myself for _____." Hold on to the paper on which your forgiveness statement is written.

Part 2 - A walk for forgiveness – I have heard when you write, read, and recite anything, it can become 90% more effective. You will be amazed at the results produced by the added deliberateness of this process. You may actually manage to let go of the past, even if you have not yet been able to do so. When they complete this exercise, many people tell me they experience a calm and quiet in their thoughts like never before.

To begin, get a garbage pail and set it where you have enough space to walk across the room from it. With your list in hand, start to walk away from the can, and for each step you take, say, "I forgive_____ for _____," loudly enough to acknowledge what you are doing. Be continually conscious of the person you are forgiving, so that no matter where they are in the world, they can feel you forgiving them.

Once you have completed the walk, close your eyes and take a moment to allow all the hurt to dissipate, watching it fade away while contemplating time passing.

Open your eyes and turn around so that you are facing your starting point by the garbage pail. Turn your paper over and slowly walk back, taking one step at a time, concentrating and focusing on yourself, and allowing any and all emotions that come up to flow freely. This time you will go down your list and say out loud, "I forgive myself for_____." Release all guilt, shame, resentment, and hurt as you go.

When you are back at the garbage pail, take your paper and rip it up while saying aloud, "I forgive myself. No more guilt. No more shame. I forgive myself." Release the pieces into the garbage.

Once you have completed the exercise, take a moment to contemplate what you just did. How do you feel?

Write down your experience and results.

_____
_____
_____
_____
_____
_____
_____

The act of forgiving yourself and others has a remarkable, positive effect on your self-confidence. Sometimes there are people that are a little harder to forgive, so we will add the compassion exercise for those instances. First, think of someone who you had a hard time forgiving in the previous exercise. Now you will use that person's name and gender in the following exercise.

Compassion Exercise

With your attention on the person you had a hard time forgiving, say the following statements aloud.

If _____ is my mirror and I have experienced sadness, then she/he must know what it is to be sad.

If _____ is my mirror and I have experienced loneliness, then she/he must know what it is to be alone.

If _____ is my mirror and I have experienced disappointment, heartache, and loss, then she/he must know what it is to be disappointed, brokenhearted, and lost.

If _____ is my mirror and I have experienced fear, then she/he must know what it is to be afraid.

If _____ is my mirror and I have experienced betrayal, then she/he must know what it is to be betrayed

If _____ is my mirror and I desire to be loved, then she/he must desire love in her/his life.

After you have completed all of these sentences, reassess your feelings toward that person. What is present for you?

RESET Principle #5 – Action

As powerful as the thoughts and words I have mentioned previously can be, they only achieve that strength because they influence our actions. Intention without action is a hope, not a truth. You must take action if you want to realize the future you have set yourself up for. I would like to share with you a short passage from the Bible, as taken from the New King James version.

> *What does it profit, my brethren, if someone says he has faith but does not have works? Can faith save him? If a brother or sister is naked and destitute of daily food, and one of you says to them, "Depart in peace, be warmed and filled," but you do not give them the things which are needed for the body, what does it profit? Thus, also faith by itself, if it does not have works, is dead.*
>
> *But someone will say, "You have faith, and I have works." Show me your faith without your works, and I will show you my faith by my works. You believe that there is one God. You do well. Even the demons believe - and tremble! But do you want to know, O foolish man, that faith without works is dead? Was not Abraham our father justified by works when he offered Isaac his son on the altar? Do you see that faith was working together with his works, and by works faith was made perfect? And the Scripture was fulfilled which says, "Abraham believed God, and it was accounted to him for righteousness." And he was*

> *called the friend of God. You see then that a man is justified by works, and not by faith only.*
>
> *Likewise, was not Rahab the harlot also justified by works when she received the messengers and sent them out another way? For as the body without a spirit is dead, so faith without works is dead also.*
>
> —James 2:14-26 NKJV

What does this passage mean? People act according to their beliefs. If you say that you believe in something but do not take any action to back that up, you are convincing no one. If you believe you can do something, you can, but part of the process is actually doing it, making it happen. If you find that you are not taking action to realize your goals, it is important to uncover the latent belief that may be present. In many cases, negative beliefs about ourselves or our capabilities lie hidden below the surface, where we are not fully aware of them. As discussed in section one, these beliefs (thoughts) can influence our actions, or lack thereof, thus preventing our goals from becoming reality.

Take action and believe in your RESET. Daily action will create the future you dream of and desire. No action, no change. It is that simple!

> **Taking massive action will give you momentum.**
>
> —Tony Robbins

Take one action step and it will create a domino effect of change. Any step in the right direction is beneficial, however, things will go more smoothly if you create a plan of action. Your action plan must be in alignment with what want to achieve. Here are some key components of a solid action plan. Think through each question and come up with an action plan for your goals. Write it down and keep it.

- What do you want to achieve?
- What is your deadline?
- Who will help you with your goal?
- What possible obstacles might arise, and how will you overcome them?
- What are some possible checkpoints along your path to success?
- What will be your opportunities to renew your commitment?

Here is one important thing to remember: Action has the word "act" in it. Take a look at yourself. Are you acting like, in essence, being, the person you wish to become? In order for me to become a world champion, I had to act like one first. As my mentor put it, I had to "try on the lifestyle." Before I ever won the title, I had to think like a champion, train like a champion, dream like a champion, walk, talk, breathe, and eat like a champion.

Without acting in this way I would never have been successful. How about you? Who are you being? Are you being the wife, husband, leader, parent, teacher, etc. that you want to be? If not, how does your behavior have to change? Are you committed to that transformation and becoming *Unbreakable*?

RESET Principle #6 – Accountability

Accountability is everything! In order to RESET for becoming *Unbreakable*, you must hold yourself accountable to someone, whether it be yourself, a friend, or a coach. Your accountability will allow you to experience your RESET mindfully, and to make the decisions you need to create the life changes you desire and deserve. Without accountability, there is no viable way to stay on course.

Consider this: Does a plane fly without a destination, flight plan, and an air traffic controller to give account to? No, it does not and neither will you. If you start on your RESET without setting up an accountability system, you can easily end up running like a hamster on its wheel, unchanging, uninspired, and unfocused, and unaware of your progress.

When determining an accountability partner, choose someone with whom you can be open, transparent, and vulnerable, but who will not judge you on your path. For many people, it is helpful to use a coach as an accountability partner, since a coach does not have any preconceived notions about you and has not been directly involved in your struggles or achievements so far. As a new part of your life, he or she should have no compunction about holding you to the highest standard you set for yourself. However, anyone who you feel fits this description can do the job if they are willing and able.

Another aspect of your accountability plan should be evaluating those with whom you surround yourself, even if they are not consciously participating in your progress. We are all heavily influenced by our surroundings, be they positive or negative.

Look around and examine your situation. How is your environment? Are you trying to organize or lead others while your own household is a disaster? With whom are you spending your time? Make a list of the 5 people with whom you spend the most time. Add up their salaries and divide it by 5 to get the average. That should equal either what you currently earn or what you want to earn.

The same goes for intelligence, ambition level, etc. If you are the smartest person in your group, you should consider hanging around with some other people. On the other hand, if you surround yourself with people who are smarter and more accomplished than you are at this point, you will constantly be learning and gaining tools for success. All aspects of your environment must be congruent with your goals, so you can stay focused on your path to a successful RESET and become *Unbreakable*.

RESETS are necessary in every area of our lives. In order to become unbreakable and have an indomitable spirit, you must RESET, REIMAGINE, and REINVENT YOUR LIFE. RESETS can happen daily, weekly, or yearly. Most of us will have small RESETS fairly often, but we can also have large life-changing RESETS, every once in a while, or regularly. RESETTING and becoming unbreakable will require courage, strength, and faith, but you are capable of whatever you set your mind and heart to. I have faith in you!

• CHAPTER 4 •

To Begin, Just Breathe

Have there been times when your life felt out of your control, and like you could never get it all done? Those are the times when you need to step back and, literally, just breathe.

The song "Breathe" by Johnny Diaz, is about the crazy kind of life we live with too much to do and all the stress that creates, but the real message, and what I'm saying here is, "Breathe, just breathe."

I know from working with students for a long time that many people "don't breathe," as strange as that may sound. *Breath* is essential to life. It gives us the power and the ability to focus and release tension. In this chapter, I will share with you a very simple breathing technique to practice daily.

Breathing is a key component of becoming *unbreakable*. First, it energizes you physically. Every cell in your body needs oxygen, so if you are slumped and breathing shallowly, you aren't taking in enough oxygen to get to all your organs. And equally importantly, breathing deeply and slowly calms your mind. It can transform how you feel and how you connect with the world around you.

The way we breathe is the way we respond, directly impacting our emotions and our responses to the pressures of life. Try to recall a time when you had been stressed or anxious, and when you had felt confident. How were you breathing during those moments? When you were feeling confident, did you notice how your breathing pattern differed from that of anxious or worried breathing?

When we feel overwhelmed, stressed, or "panicky," our breathing is shallow, rapid, and ineffective in alleviating how we feel. Sometimes we end up holding our breath and don't realize it! Now if we just take a moment to consciously deep breathe, we can reap a multitude of health benefits and effectively regain our bearing, our focus, and our confidence.

When a student comes in for a lesson and feels very stressed, I teach them to practice breathing for about thirty minutes every day. To breathe properly, we need to practice taking deep breaths from the lower abdomen. In Tai Chi, we practice this by placing the tongue on the roof of the mouth and breathing through the nose, taking full breaths from the area we call the *dan tien*, which is found two inches below the navel.

To teach this, first, I have the student lay on their back, then I place a big book or object over their abdomen. As they lay there I have them speak to me first, then ask them to be quiet and focus their attention on where they are breathing from, as well as to the rising and falling of their abdomen during each breath. The purpose of this exercise is to help them experience the sensation of the abdominal muscles being used, rather than only the chest, which is associated with nervous or anxious breathing.

The results have been very impactful. I had a student, whom I trained in Tai Chi, whose goal was to reduce her stress during her morning commute into the city to a stressful job. She loved her job and found it very rewarding despite the demands, and she did not want to switch careers. We had to find a way for her to continue, but in the most conscientious way possible, keeping in mind that stress is a silent killer if not dealt with properly.

And so, we implemented a new routine: (1) She started to take public transportation as opposed to driving in; (2) she practiced breathing for thirty minutes daily; and, (3) she incorporated meditation into her day on a regular basis. I had explained to her that for her to truly feel the benefits, Tai Chi and breathing had to be a part of her. She could not just *do* Tai Chi; she had to *be* Tai Chi.

So, what did I mean by that? Many people can *do* an activity and put in the time and practice. But when you choose to *be* something, you give it life; you give it purpose and meaning. The way you approach it would be completely different because you have committed to the process at a higher level. Before you know it, you have *become* it.

This activity that you have chosen is now a part of you and how you are experiencing the world. You are now living it through your thoughts, actions, and behavior. So, if this student became Tai Chi, she would learn how to experience her life in a calmer state and with less stress. She would be living its principles and putting them into daily practice.

Now that you know that one of the quickest ways to shift your stress level is also the easiest, you now have the power to prevent stress from breaking you. Just remember to BREATHE, and to do it softly, not forcefully. It is cost-free and can be done anywhere and anytime. Deep, full breathing expands and stretches your muscles, and, in doing so, it relaxes your joints, releasing physical tension. It also increases the flow of oxygen to the brain, feeding your brain cells so you feel more alert, focused and, refreshed— and who doesn't need these now?

In Tai Chi, because of the use of slow and purposeful movements for meditation, the breathing is not just about getting the air in an out of the lungs; it also moves oxygen through the blood and *vital energy* through various channels in the body, promoting nourishment, cleansing, repairing and energizing of the body.

Here is a quick exercise that can be done standing, seated, or lying down. When seated on a chair or standing, make sure both feet are shoulder-width apart and are flat against the floor, and your shoulders relaxed or "sunken." If standing, bend your knees slightly and just let your weight sink beneath your feet. Place your hands on your lower abdomen and close your eyes. Breathing through your nose, feel your belly expand as you inhale, and relax as you exhale. Do this for nine cycles of breath. Inhale and exhale equals one breath cycle. To be "in the moment," focus only on your breathing as you allow your whole body to relax, working your way from the top of your head to the bottom of your feet.

References

Bergland, Christopher. "Diaphragmatic breathing exercises and your vagus nerve." *Psychology Today*. Sussex Publishers, LLC. 16 May 2017. www.psychologytoday.com/blog/the-athletes-way/201705/diaphragmatic-breathing-exercises-and-your-vagus-nerve

Da, Liu. *T'ai Chi ch'uan and meditation.* Schocken Books Inc, 1986.

UNBREAKABLE

• CHAPTER 5 •

Unbreakable Legacy

If it won't matter a hundred years from now, why do it?

— *Fred Mertens*

My business mentor, *Fred Mertens*, is a great storyteller, and that was the lesson from one of his stories that I still think of often: "If it won't matter a hundred years from now, why do it?"

We all have dreams, some big, some small, but how often do we consider the impact of those dreams? Martin Luther King had a dream, and today how many millions of people enjoy the freedoms he was willing to die for? Howard Schultz, the founder of Starbucks, changed the way we think about the coffee experience. Steve Jobs changed the way we use computers and communicate. Elon Musk changed the way we think about cars. These dreamers, thinkers, and entrepreneurs changed our lives forever and a hundred years from now I am certain their contributions will not be forgotten.

How about you? What will be your legacy? What will you be remembered for a hundred years from now? What will people say about you in your eulogy? What dreams do you have that you have not pursued? What is holding you back? Whose life would change if you found the courage to live your dreams?

The Inspirational Story of Rose

Back in the summer of 2000, there was a story about a woman named Rose that went viral on Facebook. There were many different versions online, published without the author's name, but it has since been attributed to Dan Clark and it was published in 1999 as "Never Too Old to Live Your Dream" in *Chicken Soup for the College Soul*.

You may remember it, it tells of an 87-year-old woman who has always dreamed of getting a college education, and she finally does. But not only does she succeed, she shares the wisdom gained in her 87 years of living, and everyone around her benefits from that. You can find the story online, it's worth looking up.

UNBREAKABLE

A Legacy of Love

Successful people talk about it being lonely at the top. It is not lonely. Sometimes you have to go it alone, and the right people will show up to support you. However, you have to be willing to go it alone, you have to be willing to endure the silence of your own mind and your own thoughts and your own being. And within that, you will find not only courage, but the strength to keep moving forward.

The first time I truly experienced "going it alone" was when I separated from my first mentor in a very unfortunate situation. It was devastating. One of the things I learned was that my confidence was coming from outside of myself. It was wrapped up in another person's thoughts, in another person's ideas of who they thought that I could be, and not necessarily who I saw myself as.

This was a turning point for me. I realized two things. One, that the source of my confidence cannot be outside myself, except for my faith in God. Two, that confidence is fleeting.

With the pain of losing somebody who you perceived as your biggest supporter, you gain something else. You gain insight into who you are.

Little did I know that this lesson learned so early would serve me in the future....

I was to experience that devastating feeling of separation again, only this time it would be much worse. It was the loss of my best friend, Jennifer Brown, whom I lost to cancer.

From the time we met, we shared a deep bond. We spoke every day, sharing our dreams, hopes, and goals for our future lives—she knew everything about me. We were in each other's weddings; we were more than friends, we were family.

Working side by side for 25 years, running all my companies, we accomplished many things together. I remember

Jen and her husband Dave driving to Kentucky to support me when I came out of retirement to compete in the world championship. It seemed that she always had my back and I had hers.

One day, Jen told me that she believed she wasn't well. I can recall telling her she had nothing to worry about, that all would be okay; but she was right. She was not well—she had breast cancer. She got treatment and it went into remission. We thought she had it beat.

We never thought it would come back, but it did. And it had metastasized to her brain. She sent me a text on October 26th that read, "I have 3-6 months to live." I was in shock. I immediately tried to call, but she wasn't ready to talk about it. I did not want her to accept that prognosis. I told her there had to be an answer, a solution to this new information.

After experimental treatments, chemo, radiation, weeks in the hospital, then hospice at home, on November 16th she passed away.

It was like someone had torn me apart piece by piece. My heart broke. I could feel it; the pain pierced right through me like a knife. I had lost people before, but somehow this was very different. I can remember how final it was to watch as they buried her, I felt as if I took my last breath. I was not ready to say good-bye. I wanted to be strong, and keep it together, however, in that moment, I could not. The tears fell and I wanted to shout, and scream at God - WHY?!!! THIS IS SO WRONG!

All I could think about were her last words to me...I love you! She could barely get the words out because at that point she couldn't really speak anymore. When I left her house that day I did not realize that those would be the last words she would say to me.

That pain is a different kind of pain, it is a pain that really tests your resiliency, not like the pain of losing an arm or a leg, it is not a physical pain. Instead, your spirit is crushed and your faith is tested. You keep waiting on God, hoping He will come through. But what happens when His answer is "not now," or "not yet," or even "No, I have a different plan." In this moment, what do you do?

Do you wrestle with God, question or doubt Him? Or do you find a reason to keep on believing? To keep moving forward? Is it that we go through these experiences so that God can remind us that we are never alone, that He is always with us, through the good and the bad, through disasters?

Is it God's reminder that we are not alone, that he is always there, as in the poem, Footprints?

Now we know only in part, then we will know fully.
—1 Corinthians 13:12

Finding purpose has carried me through. The real question I had to ask myself is: How can I honor her legacy?

I decided that I needed to live with purpose. We had done so much and accomplished so much together, I knew what she would expect of me. It's funny how many people wanted to just fix me or say the magic words that would spring me back to the old me. I was lost for sure. I would sit and gaze out. People would talk to me and I was just not there.

All I wanted was my best friend back. I learned a lot about people over the years. I know many do not see you, they look at you, most don't want to see you as it would force them to acknowledge their own pain. I imagine the reason why: It is too unbearable for them.

What we sometimes fail to realize is that our pain can be shared, we are stronger when we lift each other up. "Strength is in unity." One afternoon I had a student who sat with me. She did not ask what most people did – "How are you?" It was as if she knew, and she did know. She shared with me her loss, and her pain. We spoke about how she got through it. She acknowledged where I was and made it all okay, normal. That is strange for me to say as I never desired to be normal – my goal in life is to be extraordinary.

Frequently in my seminars, workshops and coaching, I speak of living your life with purpose and passion. Jennifer did exactly that. If you were to ask her what her life's purpose was, she would tell you it was to love her family and friends as best as she can. In my opinion, she did that and more. She will be dearly missed.

But her spirit lives on in the way her family and friends carry her memory forward and choose to love others in the same heartfelt manner as Jennifer did. I believe her passing is a reminder to all of us to live our life and our purpose as best as we can. And this is my wish for you, to live your life with passion and purpose. The greatest measure of a life is how it is lived, so live well.

> *"God didn't promise days without pain, laughter without sorrow, or sun without rain, but He did promise strength for the day, comfort for the tears, and light for the way. If God brings you to it, He will bring you through it."*
>
> *—Unknown*

We must go beyond resilience to become *Unbreakable*.

We each live within our own story. The brain does not just observe the world, it projects a second story and that story is our perception, a perfect story that holds our life together. But when an event occurs to shatter the story, then we break. We break against these painful experiences. Then we have a choice, to remain broken or to use those pieces to start over one piece at a time and rebuild, moving forward, stronger for the experience.

When we are resilient, it just means that we are pushing it off into the future, that we can endure for a longer period of time. But when we talk about becoming unbreakable, it is reaching a place where we recognize that God has given us the ability to create a new story and the story that has ended is just a chapter in our life. And we understand that we are given the ability to create so that we can create a new story, create a new chapter, especially if we are coming from a place of possibilities.

Rewriting Your Story Exercise

In my seminars when I discuss the relationship piece, I introduce the idea of, "What is your fairytale?" Often when we struggle in relationships it is because the fairytale we have in our head does not match up with the reality of our life.

So, now I want you to recreate your story, taking the fairytale out of it, coming from a place of possibility and from this place of emptiness, sometimes maybe even brokenness. If you were to write from a place of inspiration, what would your story, your new story, look like? If you could design it to be anything you wanted it to be, if anything were possible, where would you like to be 6 months, 1 year, 2 years, 3 years, 4 years, 5 years from now? Now, go ahead and write the story...

Final Thoughts

Working through the pages of this book is simply the first step you must take to reprogram your mind and spirit to become *Unbreakable*. I have shared with you my personal challenges, triumphs and faith, in hopes it will help you to be positive, confident, and to know that you can make it through the most difficult of life experiences.

The previous pages are designed to subtly start shifting your focus from the negative to the positive, from "I am broken" to "I am healed," from "I have fallen" to "I will rise again." When you need an inspirational boost, I recommend listening to Jason Gray's "I Will Rise Again." It is a beautiful song, and I love its message, "I will rise again, stronger in the end."

Going through the book is a good start, but isn't the end of it though. You need to commit to revisiting this book as often as you can. I have heard it takes over sixteen repetitions of hearing or reading something before you get the whole message. Work through the exercises, six principles and coaching tools again for each area of your life in which you aren't thriving.

It's also important to keep in mind that no matter how much personal work you do, there will be things in life that are outside your control. Come back to the exercises in the book any time you need a reset.

I sincerely hope you not only find the champion within you, but you find the indomitable spirit that will allow you to live a fulfilling life in which you achieve your cherished dreams!

Want Help Becoming *Unbreakable*?

It is my hope that you have applied the information and done the exercises in this book with great results. The processes I gave you are often used in the beginning stages of the coaching I do, so by doing them on your own, you have given yourself a strong advantage towards achieving your goals. In addition to one-on-one coaching, I have recently added a group retreat to my program.

If you would like to learn more about how coaching and training can help you achieve your personal or business goals, and bring balance to the six key areas of your life, visit my website at www.daylighttraining.com or give us a call at (201) 888-2122 today.

About The Author

Sifu Karl Romain has led a life of adventure filled with challenges and hard-earned successes. From immigrating to the US as a child to becoming a world champion martial artist, he has had the opportunity to practice overcoming obstacles and has become *Unbreakable*.

The deep personal work he underwent during the recovery from a serious accident resulted in his interest expanding from fighting arts to healing arts and he became first a student and later a teacher of Tai Chi and Chi Gong. Karl has since taught these arts on Oprah, Dr. Oz. and the Discovery Channel, in addition to making appearances on major network news shows.

Today, Karl's purpose is to help other people become *Unbreakable*, and live the lives of their dreams. He is a certified master trainer and coach, who has been extremely successful at guiding clients through step-by-step plans and actions to help them define and achieve their goals.

His clients come from all walks of life, including business executives, entrepreneurs, pro-athletes, coaches, and couples seeking growth in their relationships. For more information on working with Karl, contact him through LinkedIn or his web page: www.daylighttraining.com.

Made in the USA
Las Vegas, NV
14 July 2024

92301639R00071